T0374368

Swoon

A very special thank you
To family, friends, lovers, thinkers
Believers and dreamers!

Swoon

AKINFE FATOU

iUniverse, Inc.
Bloomington

Swoon

Copyright © 2012 by T. N. Mitchell

All rights reserved. No part of this book may be used or reproduced by any means, graphic, electronic, or mechanical, including photocopying, recording, taping or by any information storage retrieval system without the written permission of the publisher except in the case of brief quotations embodied in critical articles and reviews.

iUniverse books may be ordered through booksellers or by contacting:

iUniverse
1663 Liberty Drive
Bloomington, IN 47403
www.iuniverse.com
1-800-Authors (1-800-288-4677)

Because of the dynamic nature of the Internet, any web addresses or links contained in this book may have changed since publication and may no longer be valid. The views expressed in this work are solely those of the author and do not necessarily reflect the views of the publisher, and the publisher hereby disclaims any responsibility for them.

Any people depicted in stock imagery provided by Thinkstock are models, and such images are being used for illustrative purposes only.

Certain stock imagery © Thinkstock.

ISBN: 978-1-4697-4650-0 (sc)
ISBN: 978-1-4697-4651-7 (e)

Printed in the United States of America

iUniverse rev. date: 03/01/2012

Carmenère

I am awakened by you
Calling me out of my
Human fabric to join yours
In a euphoric
Trance
The soundtrack of
Souls enfolded…
Liquid moans
A twin-flame
To share your life-force
With, past lives and in
This…
A lover to decide what
We shall come back as

Square of 5th's

I kiss your blood
And raise the flesh
You left behind
Remembering and
Repeating your last
Words
With a weighted heart
I yearn to feel your
Pulse on mine
Your fragrance swathes
In my aura
I tasted your skin

Sake

I want to
Unclothe a different poem
Every night, to swear by
A page to make love to
The prettiest homophones
For awkward sentences
Odd but romantic
An erstwhile lover, reworked
And evolving
Into the… longed
For and dreamed of

Alas, Forgive Me

As strong as I am...
I am fragile
I become the pieces
Strung together in
Shattering
Please gather me
I never wanted to need
You
But now...
Demoded the immaterial
Pavement
Is no longer visible
Only the paleness
That sheets it remains
In here, the volume is
Hollow
I fume to meet your
Chatter again...
But now
But, now...

Maraud

Strawflowers
Raise the dead
Seagulls hover
They'd fallen under some
Gods spell, off having
Sex religiously…
And praises going on up
In the air like hands
Demon birds honing
Hems and salvaged
Signatures as tissue
Unscathed
Run with them
Soar the highest lows
With enormity
Unto the river
Surrounded by orcas
Fallen rosin

Rewound

My life is
My favorite movie
Always moving
Reel to ink
Never a moments'
Stillness...
I am the lead...
Such brilliance
Set back on its
Scowling
And rain pummeling
Half turned leaves to
Soil
Swallowing footsteps
Wind beating branches
Snaking against my window
Nice night for your arms
Instead...
Nina Simone flaming
From the turntable

Belong

I was likely a Djeli
In another life
This one too
I story waking
In the Masai Mara
In Guinea, Senegal, Nigeria
The Serengeti maybe
Oh, how different it
Would be...
Walking in Ghana
Home...
A singing
Tribeswoman
Warrior
Samburu
Bearer of seeds
I never spoke about
Children before...

Except here...
Here is not the
Place for them

Harvest

Autumnal Equinox
The surviving butterflies
Skirt between
Neighborhood
Earth & sky
By no account
Meeting the clouds
They shall not be apart from us
Fall inaugurates, renewing
Both karmic paths & spirit
We are the last to sense the
Seasons, change
Our evening competing with
Day

Poem #954

In the heirloom garden
I make sure to leave offerings
For the ancestors and prayers
For the Creator
I'd say, they are pleased with
How divine we are
I'm fearless in my speaking
Expressive with the gestures
That follow

Oscillating carousals
I will be bringing
Cowry Shells, milk, snails
White rice and clay

Kismet

The red robin and I
Catch eyes without
Speaking, his singing
Is quite the contrary
His arrival is questionable
Having been free, captive
Then displaced, we
Know the stories
But don't mention the
Hideousness that may resurface
We burn the sun
For the remainder of our time
Staring
He hurries along with an
Obscure object removed
From the grass beds

The space offset to hymns
And pounded niceties
Is home to a colony
Of working ants, wasps and
Grasshoppers
Hands for the harvest moon
Rogue squirrels
This is the temperate place
Near the rearing womb
Warrior mother and freshly
Baked cake aromas rising
Perfume sweet flour
We sit eager to consume
The batter before the
Modern day ceremonies
Commence...
That a slice may be spared

The Other Vietnam

Black eyes, pulled hair,
Broken furniture
Childhood dreams of
A fish tank collapsing
& water pouring
Between the old wood
Downward, to the 2nd floor
Always due for fresh wounds
Aged infantry stories tell on
Landmines set off and limbs
Detaching, vodka yelling
Survives nightmares
Sacrificing sanity & self
For the
Millions of souls we will
Never know
Anger crowds out...
Some... place
Usually here
War in American homes
Death, yoke and gore

Poem 912

Our stomachs
Fed by the very beasts
We'd turn out to be
The ones we always knew
Lived inside of us
Raged and capable of
Self harming at
Hearts... beat
Then the soundlessness
Of, what have we done?
Or will do
Laments of unwanted
Evidence that will
Never hear the
Screams of day

New Life

Here I am in
The place that
Was once a prophecy
So to speak
A place where
Magnificent creators
Stirred their worlds
Into ours, making
Us aware of their
Presence

Whereabouts

An elephantine
Of city perils
Ingurgitated by a
Satirical world
Plucked and surmounted
And I'm sure you
Could tell me many
Things
But this I know by
Living it

Immersed

I.

Disobedient and
Controversial
Most of what
Is indicated
Will appear
Untitled and perhaps
Outside of the norm
Which is where
We choose to be

Electronic
Is the new language
Starring and impulsive
Fingers that could be
Used for something
More meaningful
Like skin
One day this will all
Mean something
To someone and
So on

II.

The new humans
Are quite digital
There is much
Saving and restoring
Backing up and what not
Verbiage in the new
World that all seems
Irrelevant and time
Passing...
Saline and collagen

Valleys

God made me many
Things but it isn't
By chance that poems
Live deep within
Coughed & teased out
In compelling stanzas
Not for the sake of
Form but just to
Write

$@*#!

Everything is
Going green
Except the grass
Brown, stagnant
And lifeless
Earth roaring
Open and swallowing
Itself, in the
Midst of war
And confusion
Love is the common
Thread that collects us

Evenings Like These

All the lovers
Nudging one another
Displays of affection
In public
Pretending to read
Each others palms
Sharing intimate secrets
I watch, smiling
Quietly
Searching for my
Own...

Evasive

A wounded heart
Bleeding outward
You racing from
Behind, forcing
The sword in further
I smile dangerously
As my spirit escapes
You and me...

::Forecast::

Wine & vinyl
Thunderstorm
Flame shimmering
Candle wicks
Galaxies of stars
And what not
Delicata
On countertops
An evenings' chill
Pane and poised
Victorian Drapery
Antique
Drawer pulls
Handcrafted vases
When your bedroom
Insinuates goodnight

I'll be setting sail
In the sea of
Your dreams
Beneath Egyptian
Cotton...
The satin of our
Bodies

The Eternal Beloved

In hindsight
You keep surrendering
Offering many faces
I keep meeting you
Again and again
In the heavens
All the rooms in
Every house
Placating
New promises
More passionate
Even humorous secrets
I always know
Before your lip gloss shifts
You forgive my sins
With pleasure and
I suffocate yours with
Thick sensuous verbs
Slipping beneath the
Darkness
As only... we could

To Kill A Heart

Fists break bones
Words break spirits
Eating through flesh
Lies die inside
Unwritten Senryus

Once More

The spirit of a lover
Trumpets
The very heart of the
Beloved
When lips assemble
Have not the eyes in
Their pondering
Wandered infinitely
Upon thee
Hath not the soul
In its wanting
Seized the passion
Ever spoken
We must take up
Scorched swords that
Swoon by blade
To cut down doubt
And bleed for love
If need be…

Per Saltire

There is only one us
No others exist, for if they
Did we would not, and would
Never…

There are only ones of us
Moving into a whole
None that will be
Returning from this abyss
We casted ourselves in to

No souls exiting early…
Planning for departure
On any tomorrows

It Is Rumored

For angelic sweeties
And those that wear
Their hearts on the
Invisible sleeves of
Negligee espousing the
Impressible
Confectionery feelings of
Hands abound
The divulgence of possessive
Exhalation bequeaths
Where the provocatively
Teeming textiles
Compartmentalize beside the
Discomposed aisles of
Private eyeliner,
Pump wearing, sweat
bead satires
Hosiery persuasion
Urn shattering traces of
Eau du toilette
Embracing laceless
Corset taunts…
Careful not to tease

Swoon

Tonics, good spells &
Flower essences. Come lay with me
Say and savor the sensual novelties
To be had
Then... incarnate. I miss kissing your
Chakras

You, who hath wooed my spirit
Take, take, take...
My body, instead
Of late goodbyes

Sanguine hands in the anthem of massage
Cum saturated articles of clothing
Intermingling breast
With spilled cocktails, vintage
Jazz and the ashes of cigars...
Sometimes no one has to apologize

I keep imaging navigating the
Extravagance of your vocal register
So heavenly, the gift of your
Presence

All the Spoils

A million heavens
For the first time
In a long time
I contemplated
Literary suicide
Dying the
Clean death
And being reborn

Singing and chanting
Until the sun cometh
Up

Moon rituals
Leaving ink on lingerie
Sliding poems beneath
Pillows
Relating every ballad
Played on the radio
Somehow, to you…
Whispering naughty stanzas
On the neck of, lover

The Exclaimed

How else do you explain
The changing of indigenous
Languages
The hidden beaks
And castrated tongues

Libraries, doctrines
Literature, amulets
Amputated
The tombs that have been
Removed
The sculptures stolen &
Hauled to the confinement
Of foreign museums
Bid and borrowed

Sustenance

Underneath the dimness
And the sound of wine
Slung across print
Were the speakers of
Pungent words like
Rebel and pussy
There are never
Attestants, not even
Carroty strangers
A flaunted sky unfastening
In the calm
A symphony of light
Transmuted with precision
A warm thickness
Sunk in a flowing decorum
Among angels and their
Diaphragms

We want to hear hushed tones
Ballads of solar plexus
And silhouettes
Transposed into the fold of arms
And smiles...
We want to hear

Embodiment

Timeless time is
Elapsing
As our souls rock
The good rock…
Whine and roll…
Thy as my
Ascendant
Let our bodies broil
Into matter
Lyrics and trebles
Contraptions
Bend in musicality

I, want to dance for
You
Want to dance it
Nice and slow
Arousal
Moving in close
The wilt of lilies
And sunset
Want to melt in your
Spirit
Open…
Extol the insides
Of you

Breached

Film
String of agave
And everything heavenly
Prepare your milk bath
Dip an index finger in to taste
Squeeze
The belly of
Sponge to wash away
The soapy bubbles
Streaming from
Your back, bring a
Tureen of fresh berries
Kneeling, to feed you
As you bathe
Teasing, hair from
Durable shoulders
Toweled dry

Expletive footage &
Apparatus
The credits roll
For each name
Is an erotic say
To account
Commission me

Twelve

The organic
Eyegasmic
Revelry
That can very
Well be... heard

Underneath the sleek
Arcs of feet
The lows of cobblestone
Road that have frozen...
It has not been seen...
Only by love
A way traveled
For others to find
Safely
Though few acknowledge
& replenish
Its existence

Behold

Don't you remember
The water I brought
You on the balance of
The commingled follicles
Of my afro... don't you
Remember the ceremonies

Thrones
How your garments
Were spun
And the sacredness
The sculpting
The chiseling
The molding
The praises
Your highness
You are worthy!

Supplicant

:::
::Dear One::Live In love::
:::::Remain::::In Love:::::::
:::::::::::::::::Dwell::::::::::::::::
:::

The Love Unending

I long to be breathless
In someone's arms
Enraptured
I'm not opposed to
Incomers
Encapsulate me

Hunger yearns
Want, to be sat in front
Of faux brick
With a storytellers

Legs folded… one
Under the other
Listening to lovers deepest
Secrets, the touch of
Fingertip against my
Labrum to quiet me before
I speak…
Want to be moved
Set afire
Get caught up in
Tongue of conversation

Hark

She came… for, the dialogue
Though, cold comes like a
Bride slaved to the wintery limbs
And the white carpets of lawns
Fading into the welcoming under-life
Appeased to the greeting
Pleased to see her retreat
Waving her off just as the hell noise
Of herbivores parade and drown amidst
Buildings
You have left us to shiver no more

Voices of the Sun

Zephyranthes,
Saw-tooth sunflowers,
Godsend spider lilies
Channeling
Aisles of the inner child
Seeding... potted
In an artful cylinder
Arranged near the
Lancet arch of warm
Kitchen windows
Bouquets of simplicity
And genuine hellos
Arouse, kindle and wow
The dewy magenta overtones
That bellows

Laughter shared in fond
Casual chitchat
Nestling the melancholy wilds
Of a world turned inside out
Not with coincidence,
The arduous
Fragrance that has a hand
In rearing rare succulents

At that instant
Adoration, maneuvers on me
Entertain and sway the senses
To personified exigency,
Double entendres
Converse with beauty

Second Wind

I.

Bending back across credenzas
Salted... euphoric tears of joy
Fall to taste
Echoic senses suspended in
Splendor
There is little need to hesitate
All of the skin and in... sides of you
Left cooing
Abstract artistry

II.

Spirit draws spirit
We needn't even meet
Face to face
Or speak over air waves
Our spirits seek out and
Oblige the frequency
She opened up like
Chrysanthemums
Pouring herself inside of
Me like a faucet
I shouldn't want to turn off
It is true, lover
You touch me without hands

Illustrations (II)

Impression
Grandiflora
Aflutter from asunder theme
Coated paradigms
Plum erotic magnetism
Gardened in a salted sky

Since when did such an exhilarant
Kiss end in bouts with defibrillators
Since now... when graves roll
Flung bones about the
Makeshift pine drape
When lips have died such a convincing
Death and the pucker of the
Blood that bulges behind
Them, boils in carousal

There is nothing vanilla
Resting in palates
Alive
Days exfoliate...
Cucumber sliced eyes
And caviar
On the dessert flesh
Apropos
Melodramas steadied
By the palms of a
Closet dancer
Emulsified
Antiqued, brass tub
Filled with milk...
Bizet & perhaps
Chopin

Art

A writer must be able to
Travel those parallel spaces
Between sanity, solitude, darkness
And that which isn't craft at all
An austere ephemeral encore
To put on once more
Pen, pad and sachet

Substratum

A good morning that
Awakens and shifts
Airing on the misnomers
Ousted from unpaired
Mouths'
The small things have
Distinct classifications so to
Speak…

Deliverance
Return the effervescent
Essence of my lips…
Taste them
Place them in sacred spaces
Where thank you(s) are left
Subaqueous and thus
Submarined in between
Femurs… thighs, redolence
Even bone marrow and such
Deepness thickens…
To depth
Walls and womb surrendered
Scented erudite belligerence
Oh, in an ode…
The craved satiation

Envisage

Bare muscles against muslin
The camera triggers unbeknownst
To us
Act I
Improvisation
Allow me to adjust your lighting…

Surely there is art within
The doublespeak
When… a kiss can be framed
Portrait paintings
Diagonal skylight
Imagine the touch of lust

I am no one in particular
Yet, someone to be
Remembered
Sweet all over
Induction to
An a cappella
Understructure

You have combed the
Images betiding the
Life of my bed

Poem for a Poem

Poetry, like the spirit
You must come unto
It is imparted sacredly
Keepers of a proverbial
Ancient gift

Evenings cry out to us
Others, you must sacrifice
Petition, phlebotomize and
Recede upon
Give up muses, lovers, sleep
Possessions
And affection to be in solitude
Alone, in the filth and the
Blackness of worlds
That do not exist
No tears come for the
Keepers of the craft
Such sorcery
To live and die as a Poet

Good Morning, Evening
Acts I & II

Followed like pleasingly
Organized chapters
They are one in the
Same
Owning them… selves
Polar and distilled
Quantum, except
Blount
Nearly righteous
Love drunken
Practicalities

There are but
A hand full of
Personalities
Perfect for shelves
Compatible maybe
Unpredictability is
More of interest
It swans in aroma
As opposed to
Cyclical fallacious
Stench

City Love Affair

I.

An attraction
To skyscrapers
Pressing deadlines
Underworlds and
Underpasses
An epode to
Phallic symbols
The illustrious
Caviling and the
Sentimental
A concrete
Romance
God and
Literature
The prestige of
Persistence

II.

Phenomenal mind
Enchanted, breath
Swept sex
Were to feel the beat
Of ostrich feather
Titter tatter and
Daffodil limbs contort
The embrace of tonsils
Tango swaying
Absorbed by the
Viticulture
Haute-Medoc of
A lifetime
Well spent chasing
Innocence

Change Changes

Living out of bags for
Weeks
Red mod sofa bed
Dressed in lint and
Moderate Bombay
Cat dander, wearing a
Slender grin ear to ear
I will remember every
Light prism, inch of
Architecture, river, pier
And bridge
Lest not to say goodbye
Lastly finding my destination

Life changes like
Overhead subways…
Tracks and the passing
Of screeching between
Mammoth buildings

Advent
In the contour of
Willows brush
Percolate
Sunken in tides of
Dream catchers
And the wickers she
Goes on about
The dark light
Within
The heels of
Rhythms reason
Dancing the outskirts
And interlopers alike
Taking me higher
I love every
Thread of you

Not Withstanding...

Spellbound nights spent
Self dining in
Irish pubs
Vowing to
Not die alone
Hearing the unprecedented
Chatter of every voice
All at once and then
Isolated conversations
Luckily
I make nothing of it...

Transfixed

The thrill of success
Burns good
Savage like
Fuck noises
From ligament to
Ligament
And the loudest
Internal scream
Sweet but
What does it mean?
To have, it...

In Transit

Romance is
Riding commuter
Trains to and fro
Thinking of lover...
Gazing each city as
It passes forcefully
Remembering the
Trees glazed in
Snowflakes
Past colloquy
Roof tops too, and
Ledges white
I am with color
And more powerful
Than you know...

Static

Not as vacant as empty
A voice reaches over me
A cigarette lit
Door screeched open
Instructions echo...
Losing leverage
The handles turn
Brows cringe
What lies beneath
The layers of
Mascara
Sometimes arguments
Erupt like blown out
Brown paper bags
Nothing orchestral
By its crumbling
The air going in and
Out of lungs like a
Clarinet

Replicate

Don't sell me scriptures
I like lit undigested,
Uncontained enigmas
Swift canvas
Blots
Suspended, expanding
Intestines
I will wear an apron
For you
Carefully drizzling
The ambience of tomato,
Basil and caper vinaigrette
Over halibut
Slowly, burying
Freshly steamed leeks
In its wake
The Riesling awaits
Unexpected Longevity

The beginning of
Something yet
Defined, not awkward
Misguided... ill shaped
The bountiful
Pleasantry of stream
Flailing birth
Chants from stones
Stillness donating
Itself to the fullness
Of frog bellies
Vowels

Encounter

Defining mind twist
Syrupy sweet fluid
Warm in spiraled chocolate
Idolatry
Attentive reaction to a
Multiplicity of emotions
Neither penetration nor the
Verbal pulling of lungs
Internally... turned on
Filling splashes of tongue
Heavy against walls
Sucking of discreet genes
Broadcasting mental zeniths
Over finely transcribed pores
And you impregnated with
Badly behaved thoughts

Lover Do Come

By your alchemy
I would clam up in your
Skin and say speechless
Repeatedly
We would be married
To the thought of
It all
By the ending of
The songs
Favored song...
Seeing the
The air fluctuate
A sidereal margin

I feel you above
Simulating
Pond on moist
Soil and the
Footsteps led
To it
The borrowed
Mornings we
Encapsulate

And So On...

Eros (Part II)

A stranger to my own
Skin though the void
Of foreignness
Entering my
Good place again
Pounding me
Further into a
Self ordained hell
A prisoner
Feeling myself
Still, silently
Rushing the end
Now when she
Collides against me
Alive and vibrant
With smiles
Of satiation
I feel my secret

Slip away from
Me in the passion
Of fingertips
Pressed
Taking my mouth
Completely with
A swipe of her
Love quickly
Like a hurricane
Swung in debris
Mustering from
My being...

The worlds disdain
Falls on me
Yet my want is
Evident

She Too Is Desirable

Like his many
Coming women
Through revolving
Doors…
I endured
But lying on her
Breast such as
He had
Divorcing the
Predictable
Scruff of his
Mustache and
Harsh outdated
Cologne
Her flesh tells
Me why he
Was unfaithful…
She has become
Irresistible even to
Myself

Under-Poem

You brought me to
You like a cold reading
Stumbling over myself
Fucking up every line
Tip toeing the balance
Beam or hanging in the
Lack thereof
Somewhat like an
Inner fire lying
In the cloves
Of my esophagus
I am afraid to
Swallow the knot
That has woven
Itself in my throat
Loosening that reality
Between what was
And is to come
A kind of fate that
Has no faith
Only questions
Because trust and
Believing are two
Different things…
Right?

Swab

Deep into the
Unknown
Roses unravel
And disincarnate
Into damned sweat
Right before our
Eyes
Your saliva dangling
From the hinges of
Your lips

And I gave
All of thee
All of the me there
Was to give
In that moment
Your remarks cut like
A knife... and I
Was willing to
Hemorrhage
For you
Watch the speckles
Dabble scuffled paper
The accuser and the
Curser

An Evenings Breath

In the blurred evenings
Where the crack of sky
Is married to the clouds
And sunset
I, myself love to walk the
Nights amidst the street lights
And strange faces
Allowing the wings of bugs
To crackle beneath
My feet like fire
Being put out
A.M. hours
I came to be the
Beat of DJ
Scratches
Bartered volume
Resuscitation

Our flesh has no
Beginning, nor ending
Just the indent of
Desperation

Tactual
Togetherness
The foreign nuances of
The outside world is finally
Silenced
Your finger tips…
Lips, swept against mine
Your nudity autographs
My chest
The pressure
Of containing a yelling
Heartbeat
In pleasure
Implodes
In the excitable joy
Of the unscripted

Quay (Version II)

When enamored
Mannerisms
And gestures can no
Longer be contained
In the oval of
Discussion...
That is when eyes
Come in close
And a soft
Index finger
Moves over lips
To quiet the
Short anxious breaths
Like the night songs
Of small innocent insects
Drowning in the black
Dimensions beneath park
Benches and
Provocative whispers
Then no words at all
Heat springing in and
Out of pores

Starseeds

Like a thunderously decanting
Rainstorm or God mouth spelling down
Youth shakes the core, the roots
Branches of fervor, the sky carpet and
Starlets fall onto faces
Enjoining themselves to the chary notches
Of cement with lips a pucker
What relevance convinces outliers
Of horizontal hereafters
Prearranged, in and
Out of wistfulness
Perusing the papery stages
Come
Lay me upon your altar
Esoteric lover
Rework, exert and comfort me

The Immovable

Uncouth dead flowers
Resurface by the earnest of
Crude beginnings of
An uncomely garden and
Less than decorative cement
Snarling
With prudent weeds
Returning again when
The ceilings are full with
Inelegant funk and valiant
Oaths
Cinderblocks overcome
By rodents leavings
Spider webbings
No house guest
Permitted

The Uncertainty

Comfy colors of Fall
Upon us
Your voice still wails
The well-known
No one speaks
Otherwise
The bed still boasts
Your imprint
Spare slippers and
Empty housecoats
Cold... awaits
You never come
Quite the same...
Upsides of small
Picture frames
Cramp the
Charred hallways
Those fingers
That sailed
The scaly drywall
Vacant and void
Always searching
For more

Rehearsal

On again off again
Consonant...
I would take you
Back a thousand
Times, each one
Forgetting the reasons
You left, and why...

Demigods

I do not suggest, that
I have ever forgotten
The strength of our brothers
Shoulders, always
Lifting us higher
Skipping rocks through
Abandoned creeks
All of the
Shrieking in our houses
Hushing the wolves
Clawing

Be Overcome

Fingers rinsed
Beneath the
Waterfall
Of your hair
Massaged by
Each delightful
Strand
You, who hath
Pilfered the
Columns
Of my heart
I am content
In the winds
Sands and
Shadows
I will not be

Needing
It back
It now pulsates
Inside
Of you
I blush each time
You breathe
I fall for you
Like a night with the
Perfect moon
Your body is my
Manuscript
Imprinting
In all of your
Sacred places

Granted

The last time we fucked
And made love
Was....
And I've been searching for
That high ever since

Mousquetaire

Anonymity is sexy
A bit of androgyny
Hand wanderings
Tongues in conference
Bondage &
Fondling
A confidant
Epicure

Our nakedness
Insinuates
Exponential
Sexual chemistry

Watching your
Clothing carousel
Below your ankles
Delicate toffee
Kisses on each eye lid
The body
An exotic odyssey
To orbit in its

Entirety
Entry and erogenous
Regions to explore
Anatomically
Opera gloves
Extended
Parasols afloat
Gowns pirouetting
Along the ballroom
Peering
Spaghetti straps
Yelling the
Acronyms of my
Name
A Litany of phalanges
The warm mist of clitoris
That swells and welcomes
Cool adhesive apertures
Your sugary compote
Your pheromones alone
Enchanted… seduced me

Chartered

I miss the kiss of your voice
Your lips speaking on me
Let us converse in tongues...

Thighs butterfly open
Like a tulip
Over a crowded alter
All but wax
Contained atop it
And the palms
That usually meet
In prayer... streak
Along velvet caramel

Embalming a living
Body with saliva

African Cucumber

I am the storm that
Destroys the shore
The violent waves
That catches the wind
In its midst
Returning them from
Whence it came
The eternal extinguisher
Of fire

When you see queens
Standing in all
Their glory, virtuous
And infinite
Exuding their power....

Bow
My greatness... is not
Up for discussion
Does not require your
Approval or validation
Will not be subject
To your questioning
By any definition
My crown & my throne

My divine right is not yours
To revoke or to challenge
Brown child of the Nile

Vocable

I am your mantra
Coming off of tongue
Like the curl of sensual
Phonetics
I take in the wetness of
Your kiss
With baited breath

Transcription

On my pillow is where
I left dreams of you
Quiet. Softly. There.

Languedoc

Above all
I am just a woman
Wanting…
To share my world
With you

Zuccotti Park

I have been introduced
To more lovely strangers
Then I dare know
Protests, protests protest
And peaceful resistance
Skeletons being
Carried out arms and
Legs
Tents romped too
We were going on about
Civil liberties, ending wars
And yelling
March quite frequently
Officers took to them
Like puppets
They creaked up

The graves
We buried ourselves
In continually
Occupying everything
We are only
What our lovers
Believe we are
Either the ripened
Pears or the shedding
Of their greed
Torpedoing down
Liberty Street...
Dogs and riot gear
We move in love and
Have no fear

Firth

My tongue swimming
Your cold breath
The softer side of your voice
Turbulence
A tour of all the ceilings

A table of almond and rice cheeses
Bordeaux and Chilean wines
To my liking
My lips have seen your body
A thousand times
A mouth that has yet to find flaw
Scores of variegated colors
The sweet after taste
Gazelle
You are invited

And All The Stars

All this talk of quantifying
Our consciousness and
Plans to get out of
Getting out
Had me flamed
Then our mouths let on
That we bless
Each others cells like
We were planets
And hypernovas again

Thermodynamics
(2nd Law Of)

We're all wondering
Praying about the
Economy and
The dwarfing dollar
We'd best learn from
Our elders
Quickly
How to create and
Mind our own
Like they warned
Us long ago
They were right
We have seen it with our
Very own tearful eyes
Less farms, more wars
So much uncertainty to
Be certain of